W9-BGY-993

Contents

Introduction

When looking for metaphors for life, we often fall back on that old standby "Life is a roller coaster." It's an apt comparison, what with life's ups and downs, its twists and turns. If a given year in our lives is like a roller coaster, however, the year 1972 was a roller coaster a mile high, and we rode it in the dark. In a thunderstorm. Without seat belts. It was one of the most tumultuous years in American history.

President Richard M. Nixon was the dominant figure in the events that unfolded in 1972, with both triumph and difficulty following in the wake of his every move. In one of the most groundbreaking moves of his or any other chief executive's career, he traveled to the People's Republic of China, opening relations with that country for the first time in the 22 years since it had gone over to Communist rule. Nixon's visit got the ball rolling to open trade relations and information exchanges between China and the United States, and it is considered a milestone in international diplomacy and the high point of Nixon's long career in public service.

In another part of Asia, however, Nixon's foreign policy was not faring as well. America's long participation in the war between North and South Vietnam had begun to run its course. Peace negotiations between North Vietnam and the United States had been going on for years in Paris, with neither side able to gain ground and with frequent walkouts. Following up on a pledge to the American people, Nixon began withdrawing American ground troops from the region while simultaneously stepping up the air war. Some of the worst aerial bombings of the war took place, and Nixon was catching his own flak as the conflict continued to drag on.

It did not help that 1972 was a presidential election year. Though the Democratic challenge proved to be weak, the president looked for ways to undermine his opposition at every turn. When operatives in the employ of the White House came to him with a scheme to use reelection campaign funds to conduct illicit surveillance and sabotage on Democratic candidates and party leaders, Nixon approved the plan.

Donnie,
Happy 40th birthday!
To the man that god has
blessed me + my children
with. I am so glad we found
each other + so happy that
we made it thru everything

The Year in History

1972

Your
Loving
Wife
Duane
7/20/2012

Whitman Publishing, LLC

www.whitman.com

© 2012 Whitman Publishing, LLC

3101 Clairmont Rd., Suite G, Atlanta GA 30329

Correspondence concerning this book may be directed to the publisher at the address above, attention: The Year in History: 1972.

ISBN: 0794837328

Printed in China

Scan the QR code at left or visit us at www.whitman.com for a complete listing of collectibles-related books, supplies, and storage products.

Whitman®

While it may not have been the only time, before or since, that such "dirty tricks" have been part of an election cycle, in this particular case the plan had two major flaws: the job was handled badly, and there was a leak in the conspiracy. Though in 1972 Nixon won reelection in one of the most decisive landslides in political history, two years later he would be forced to resign the presidency in disgrace.

The year 1972 had its roller-coaster moments outside the Beltway as well. The Olympic Games in Munich, West Germany, would prove the site of many triumphs but also of a horrific tragedy as Palestinian terrorists stormed the Olympic village and killed several Israeli athletes, sparking a shadow war as Israeli intelligence operatives spent the remainder of the year carrying out acts of revenge. A ceasefire between British forces and the Irish Republican Army on the streets of UK-controlled Northern Ireland was broken by the massacre known as "Bloody Sunday." For the last time, astronauts walked on the moon.

At the same time, this was an amazing year for entertainment. The Rolling Stones and Neil Young both released what are considered the best albums of their careers; George Harrison assembled a stellar group of performers in the Concerts for Bangladesh, the world's first all-star benefit super-concert; and David Bowie arrived on American stages for the first time. The Miami Dolphins became the only team in NFL history to go from opening day to the Super Bowl without a loss. And *The Godfather*, a film that almost didn't get made because of concerns about its criminal protagonists, opened to more box-office sales than any movie ever made before.

This was a year that changed everything: the relationships between nations, the way we make and receive art, and the nature of the presidency itself. Some of us left the roller coaster sick and wobbly, some exultant, but all of us were transformed by the ride.

Born on August 30 in San Diego, California, Cameron Diaz would become an award-winning actress with her own star on the Hollywood Walk of Fame.

Famous People Born in

1972

The list of celebrities born in 1972 constitutes an interesting cross-section of the world of entertainment, sports, and the arts that dominates our popular imagination today. This is not the generation that started hip-hop, the last original art form in America, but it is the one that helped to propel it to the heights at which it currently sits, with legends like Busta Rhymes, Eminem, and the Notorious B.I.G. all born in 1972. Some of the biggest acts in alternative and country music were also born in this year, as well as the players in some of the most popular films and television shows we view.

The array of sports figures on this list is surprising in its depth and greatness, especially when we consider how many of them have already retired from their respective sports after setting and breaking records. Mia Hamm, regarded as the best female soccer player the sport has ever seen, is on this list, as well as baseball phenom Shawn Green and the indomitable Shaquille O'Neal.

When a certain time or place produces a large number of extraordinary people, people like to say there must be something in the water. If that's the case, then the year 1972 was a veritable monsoon.

Shaquille O'Neal, born on March 6 in Newark, New Jersey, would become an NBA basketball star.

January 1—Catherine McCormack, stage and film actress *(Braveheart, Dangerous Beauty)*

January 1—Maile Maloy, author *(A Family Daughter)*

January 11—Amanda Peet, television and film actress *(Saving Silverman, Studio 60 on the Sunset Strip)*

January 13—Nicole Eggert, television actress *(Baywatch)*

January 18—Mike Lieberthal, baseball catcher (Philadelphia Phillies)

February 8—Whitney Gaskell, novelist *(Pushing 30)*

February 11—Craig Jones, keyboardist (Slipknot)

February 11—Kelly Slater, professional surfer (11-time world surfing champion)

February 14—Drew Bledsoe, football quarterback (New England Patriots)

February 14—Rob Thomas, singer (Matchbox 20)

February 15—Jaromir Jagr, hockey right winger (Philadelphia Flyers)

February 16—Jerome Bettis, football halfback (Pittsburgh Steelers)

February 17—Billie Joe Armstrong, singer and guitarist (Green Day)

February 24—Manon Rheaume, hockey goaltender (the only woman to play in the NHL)

February 29—Antonio Sabato Jr., television actor *(General Hospital)*

March 6—Shaquille O'Neal, basketball center and commentator (Los Angeles Lakers)

March 10—Matt Kenseth, NASCAR driver (Winston Cup 2003)

March 13—Common (born Lonnie Rashid Lynn Jr.), hip-hop artist *(Finding Forever)*

March 17—Mia Hamm, soccer forward (World Cup champion, Olympic gold medalist)

March 17—Paige Hemmis, television host *(Extreme Makeover: Home Edition)*

March 18—Dane Cook, comedian *(Retaliation)*

March 22—Cory Lidle, baseball pitcher (Oakland A's)

March 22—Elvis Stojko, Olympic silver medalist in figure skating

March 28—Nick Frost, actor *(Shaun of the Dead)*

April 3—Jennie Garth, television actress *(Beverly Hills 210)*

April 4—Jill Scott, singer-songwriter *(Who Is Jill Scott?)*

April 6—Jason Hervey, television actor *(The Wonder Years)*

April 11—Jason Varitek, baseball catcher (Boston Red Sox)

April 17—Tony Boselli, football offensive tackle (Jacksonville Jaguars)

April 17—Jennifer Garner, film and television actress *(Alias, 13 Going on 30)*

April 18—Eli Roth, film director and actor *(Hostel)*

April 20—Carmen Electra, television actress and singer *(Baywatch)*

April 20—Stephen Marley, reggae singer and son of Bob Marley

April 24—Chipper Jones, baseball third baseman (Atlanta Braves)

Future actress Rebecca Romijn is born on November 6 in Berkeley, California.

April 29—Derek Mears, stuntman *(Friday the 13th)*

May 1—Julie Benz, television actress *(Angel, Dexter)*

May 2—Dwayne Johnson, professional wrestler (as "The Rock") and film actor *(The Scorpion King)*

May 20—Busta Rhymes (born Trevor Tahiem Smith, Jr.), hip-hop artist *(The Big Bang)*

May 21—The Notorious B.I.G., aka Biggie Smalls (born Christopher George Latore Wallace, d. 1997), hip-hop artist *(Life After Death)*

May 30—Manny Ramírez, baseball left fielder and designated hitter (Boston Red Sox)

May 30—Dave Roberts, baseball center fielder and coach (San Diego Padres)

June 2—Wayne Brady, comedian *(Whose Line Is It Anyway?)*

June 2—Wentworth Miller, television actor *(Prison Break)*

June 4—Derian Hatcher, hockey defenseman (Dallas Stars)

June 5—Chuck Klosterman, journalist and author *(Sex, Drugs and Cocoa Puffs)*

June 7—Karl Urban, film actor *(Star Trek)*

June 12—Bounty Killer (born Rodney Basil Price), reggae artist *(My Xperience)*

June 12—Robin Tunney, television and film actress *(The Craft)*

June 15—Andy Pettitte, baseball pitcher (New York Yankees)

June 16—John Cho, film actor *(Harold and Kumar Go to White Castle)*

June 29—Samantha Smith, peace activist who wrote a famous letter to Soviet premier Yuri Andropov about nuclear war

July 1—Claire Forlani, film actress *(Mystery Men, Meet Joe Black)*

July 2—Darren Shan, author (the *Cirque du Freak* series)

July 7—Lisa Leslie, basketball center (Olympic gold medalist)

July 10—Sofia Vergara, film and television actress *(Modern Family)*

July 22—Keyshawn Johnson, football wide receiver (Tampa Bay Buccaneers)

July 23—Marlon Wayans, actor, producer, writer, and comedian *(White Chicks, G.I. Joe: The Rise of Cobra)*

July 27—Maya Rudolph, television and film actress and comedienne *(Saturday Night Live, Bridesmaids)*

July 28—Elizabeth Berkley, television and film actress *(Saved by the Bell, Showgirls)*

July 29—Wil Wheaton, television actor *(Star Trek: The Next Generation)*

August 6—Geri Halliwell, British singer (Spice Girls)

August 10—Angie Harmon, television actress *(Law & Order)*

August 14—Ed O'Bannon, basketball power forward (UCLA Bruins)

August 15—Ben Affleck, film actor, director, writer, and producer *(Good Will Hunting)*

August 16—Emily Robison, multi-instrumentalist (Dixie Chicks)

Brad Paisley, born on October 28 in Wheeling, West Virginia, would grow up to be a highly successful country musician—even entertaining the president and first lady of the United States.

August 25—Marvin Harrison, football wide receiver (Indianapolis Colts)

August 30—Cameron Diaz, film actress *(Charlie's Angels, Being John Malkovich)*

August 31—Chris Tucker, film actor and comedian *(Rush Hour)*

September 6—Idris Elba, English film and television actor *(The Wire, Luther)*

September 6—China Mieville, English author *(Perdido Street Station)*

September 6—Anika Noni Rose, Tony Award–winning actress *(Caroline, or Change)*

September 8—David Arquette, film actor *(Scream)*, producer, and wrestler

September 8—Lisa Kennedy Montgomery, radio host and MTV VJ
    (Alternative Nation)

September 9—Goran Visnjic, Croatian film and television actor *(ER)*

September 17—Bobby Lee, comedian *(Mad TV)*

September 21—Liam Gallagher, singer (Oasis)

September 23—Jermaine Dupri, music producer (Destiny's Child, Mariah Carey)

September 26—Shawn Stockman, singer (Boyz II Men)

September 27—Gwyneth Paltrow, film and television actress
    (Shakespeare in Love, Glee)

October 5—Grant Hill, basketball forward (Phoenix Suns)

October 17—Eminem (born Marshall Bruce Mathers III), hip-hop artist
    (The Slim Shady LP)

October 21—Saffron Burrows, film and television actress *(Boston Legal)*

October 23—Jimmy Wayne (born Jimmy Wayne Barber), country singer
    (Do You Believe Me Now)

October 28—Terrell Davis, football running back (Denver Broncos)

October 28—Brad Paisley, singer and guitarist *(5th Gear)*

October 29—Tracee Ellis Ross, television actress *(Girlfriends)*

October 29—Gabrielle Union, film actress *(Bring It On)*

November 1—Toni Collette, Australian actress *(The Sixth Sense)* and singer

November 1—Jenny McCarthy, television actress and model *(Singled Out)*

November 6—Thandie Newton, film actress *(The Pursuit of Happyness)*

November 6—Rebecca Romijn, model and film actress *(X-Men)*

November 8—Gretchen Mol, film actress *(The Notorious Bettie Page)*

November 10—Shawn Green, baseball right fielder (Los Angeles Dodgers)

November 14—Josh Duhamel, film and television actor *(Transformers: The Movie)*

November 15—Jonny Lee Miller, English film actor *(Trainspotting, Mansfield Park)*

December 15—Stuart Townsend, Irish film actor *(The Queen of the Damned)*

December 19—Alyssa Milano, television actress *(Charmed)*

December 19—Warren Sapp, football defensive tackle (Tampa Bay Buccaneers)

December 29—Jude Law, Academy Award–nominated film actor *(Cold Mountain)*

December 31—Joey McIntyre, singer (New Kids on the Block)

What to choose? With a strong economy and a strong dollar, consumers had many choices of things to buy, and the money to buy them.

The **Cost** of **Living** in
1972

The year 1972 brought an economic surge as the Dow Jones topped 1,000 for the first time in the nation's history. While the nation kept a weather eye on inflation, the economic crisis of the 1970s was still a couple of years off, and we were willing to spend on the plethora of new consumer goods appearing in stores.

Digital technology started to take hold with the advent of the handheld calculator and the digital watch, made possible by advances in LED displays. Unknown to most people, there was even a filmless digital camera, though it lay far beyond the average shopper's reach. We did, however, have a new innovation from Polaroid in the stores: an inexpensive camera that kicked out photos that developed themselves.

In 1972 *TV Guide* magazine stopped designating programming as "color," because by that time most homes in America had color televisions. Now the special designation was saved for programs in black and white, and those were scarce. The average American home enjoyed the most up-to-date technology and affordable consumer goods, and despite the turbulence going on in the rest of the world, the majority of us were doing well.

Jewelry-store owner Mike Cross makes tie tacks, earrings, and paper weights from polished chunks of oil shale.

Statistics about American life in 1972:

The average American's yearly **income** was $11,800.

The minimum **wage** was $1.60 per hour.

Median income **tax** was 23.3%.

The annual rate of **inflation** in the U.S. was 3.27%

At the end of the year the **Dow Jones** Industrial Average was 1,020.

The average cost of a new **house** was $27,550.

The average monthly **rent** was $165.

Household appliances and furniture:

17-cubic-foot refrigerator: $288.88

Gas range: $199.00

Washing machine: $169.00

Clothes dryer: $119.00

Toaster: $15.95

Fondue set: $13.88

7-piece bedroom set: $498.00

10-piece dining room set: $888.00

3-piece living room set: $488.00

Twin-size mattress: $34.50

Bed sheets: $5.00

Blanket: $10.00

Mickey Mouse alarm clock: $9.95

Swing set with lawn glider and slide: $58.99

Electronics:

Home stereo: $116.95

8-track tape player: $49.95

Cassette tape player: $24.50

15" color television: $329.95

12" black-and-white portable television: $97.95

Kodak pocket camera: $30.00

Polaroid Land Camera: $19.95

8-digit electronic calculator: $98.95

Groceries:

Dozen eggs: 52 cents

Gallon of milk: $1.20

8-oz. loaf of bread: 33 cents

Pound of butter: 75 cents

Pound of bacon: 83 cents

A mother and daughter return
home from a grocery-shopping
trip in Chicago.

Pound of hamburger: 64 cents
5-lb. bag of sugar: 50 cents
5-lb. bag of potatoes: 59 cents
3-lb. bag of apples: 47 cents
10 Florida oranges: 55 cents
Pound bag of yellow onions: 9 cents
Can of Campbell's tomato soup: 10 cents
18-oz. box of corn flakes: 37 cents
Pound box of Oreo cookies: 49 cents
Hershey bar: 10 cents
Six-pack of Pepsi: 69 cents

Household goods:

36-count bottle of aspirin: 26 cents
36-count bottle of Alka-Seltzer: 89 cents
150-count jar of Rolaids: $1.09
60-count package of Band-Aids: 46 cents
100-count bottle of vitamins: $1.99
18-count box of Brillo pads: 45 cents
1-quart bottle of Joy dishwashing liquid: 75 cents
Half-gallon bottle of Wisk laundry detergent: $2.64

Clothing:

Men's suit: $70.00
Men's dress shirt: $6.99
Pair of men's slacks: $20.00
Pair of jeans: $12.00
Cotton dress: $43.00
Skirt: $14.00
Pantsuit: $19.95
Girl's dress: $7.95
Pair of sneakers: $4.00

Other purchases:

New car: $3,000.00
Gallon of gas: 55 cents
First-class postage: 8 cents
Ticket for a seven-day Bermuda cruise: $575.00
Basketball: $6.99
Child's bicycle: $36.88

In December 1972, Apollo 17 astronauts Eugene Cernan and Harrison Schmitt spend about 75 hours on the Moon, in the Taurus-Littrow valley, while colleague Ronald Evans orbits overhead.

Day-by-Day Calendar of
1972

A s with any year, looking at events from 1972 on a day-to-day basis is a bit like drinking from a firehose. So much went on in the arenas of world politics, popular entertainment, sports, crime, and war that it can be a bit overwhelming to see it all at once. People like to look at past years and describe them as "a simpler time," but a glance back at 1972 reveals that the time was anything but simple.

The calendar is dominated by the movements of President Richard M. Nixon and his staff, understandable in a year that brought us the historic trip to China, the machinations of the Watergate scandal, a presidential election, and the ongoing action of the Vietnam War. But as we will see, much was going on in all other corners of the world as well. This year saw the end of the space race that had dominated the 1960s as the first man-made object left our solar system, the last two missions to the moon were completed, and the president announced the next phase of our adventure in space, the space shuttle. We can see the rise of OPEC and the stirrings of what will become an international battle over the price of oil. In sports it was a particularly spectacular year for professional football, as some of the greatest games ever played and one of the greatest teams, the 1972 Miami Dolphins, dominated our attention on Sundays. The drama of the Munich Olympics unfolded before our eyes. And it was a milestone year for women as the military, law enforcement, the sports world, and Congress itself made huge strides toward equal pay and consideration between the sexes.

That's a lot to take in, but it's all fascinating as we look back at the events that made 1972 a year never to be forgotten.

JANUARY 1

Kurt Waldheim is sworn in as secretary-general of the United Nations. He will serve until 1981 and become president of Austria in 1986, during which election his service in German intelligence during World War II will bring heavy scrutiny upon him.

JANUARY 2

First Lady Pat Nixon arrives in Liberia to begin an eight-day tour of Africa.

JANUARY 3

American space probe *Mariner 9* begins to provide the first maps of the surface of Mars.

JANUARY 4

The Hewlett-Packard HP-35, the first handheld scientific calculator capable of performing higher math functions, is introduced at a list price of $395.

JANUARY 5

President Nixon announces that NASA engineers will begin work on a reusable spacecraft called a "space shuttle."

JANUARY 6

Jerry Lee Lewis has the number one country single
in America with "Will You Take a Chance on Me?"

JANUARY 7

President Nixon formally announces that he will run for reelection.

JANUARY 8

"Brand New Key" by Melanie is the number one pop song in America.

JANUARY 9

The largest ocean liner ever built, the RMS *Queen Elizabeth,* popularly known
as the "QE2," catches fire and is destroyed while harbored in Hong Kong.

JANUARY 10

Former vice president Hubert Humphrey, President Nixon's opponent in
the 1968 election, criticizes Nixon's handling of the Vietnam War, saying it
is taking longer for Nixon to withdraw troops than it took to defeat Hitler.

JANUARY 11

Merle Haggard's "Carolyn" tops the country charts.

JANUARY 12

The U.S. Department of Labor issues its first orders restricting exposure to asbestos, an insulation material found to be carcinogenic.

JANUARY 13

George Wallace, Democratic governor of Alabama, announces his candidacy for president of the United States.

JANUARY 14

The Reverend Jesse Jackson and others form the activist organization People United to Save Humanity (PUSH).

JANUARY 15

Emergency!, a weekly television drama about paramedics and doctors, makes its debut on NBC.

JANUARY 16

The Dallas Cowboys roll over the Miami Dolphins 24–3
to win Super Bowl VI in New Orleans, Louisiana.

The 37th president of the United States, Richard Nixon (1969–1974).

JANUARY 17

Betty Smith, author of *A Tree Grows in Brooklyn,* dies at age 75.

JANUARY 18

Clarence Earl Gideon dies at age 61. His case before the U.S. Supreme Court, *Gideon v. Wainwright,* guaranteed the obligation of the state under the Sixth Amendment to provide legal counsel to defendants unable to afford such counsel themselves.

JANUARY 19

A group of entrepreneurs announces that they have created their own nation in the South Pacific by piling tons of sand atop an underwater reef. The Republic of Minerva lasts for about five months before the artificial island is annexed by the nearby nation of Tonga.

JANUARY 20

The Organization of Petroleum Exporting Countries (OPEC) raises the price of oil to $2.49 a barrel, a jump of more than 8%. This is the first of several price hikes that will contribute to the energy crisis of the mid-1970s.

JANUARY 21

The Rolling Stones' Keith Richards comes onstage to play with Chuck Berry at the Hollywood Palladium, but Berry kicks him off for playing too loud. Berry later claims not to have recognized Richards.

JANUARY 22

Louis Farrakhan, top figure and future leader of the
Nation of Islam, delivers a speech in praise of the men who
assassinated Malcolm X in 1965, angering many in the movement.

JANUARY 23

The Pro Bowl is played in Los Angeles, with the American Football
Conference beating the National Football Conference 26–13.

JANUARY 24

Pakistani prime minister Zulfikar Ali Bhutto orders
scientists to begin work on nuclear weapons.

JANUARY 25

Shirley Chisholm, the first black woman elected to Congress, announces
that she is throwing her hat in the ring for president of the United States.

JANUARY 26

Don McLean's "American Pie" tops the pop singles chart.

JANUARY 27

Gospel legend Mahalia Jackson dies at age 61.

JANUARY 28

President Nixon signs an executive order establishing the Office for Drug Abuse Law Enforcement. This will later merge with the Office of National Narcotics Intelligence to become the Drug Enforcement Administration.

JANUARY 29

G. Gordon Liddy, head of the Special Investigations Unit known as the "White House Plumbers," proposes Operation Gemstone, an extensive campaign of "dirty tricks" to be implemented against President Nixon's enemies. Among these strategies is a plan to wiretap the offices of the Democratic National Committee.

JANUARY 30

In what will become known as "Bloody Sunday," British soldiers open fire on protesters in Derry, Northern Ireland, killing 14.

JANUARY 31

The Federal Aviation Administration orders all U.S. airlines to begin screening passengers and their luggage for weapons before allowing them to board flights.

FEBRUARY 1

The Carpenters' "Hurting Each Other" is the number
one single on the adult-contemporary chart.

Shirley Chisholm (D-N.Y.), the first African-American woman elected to Congress, announces
her candidacy for president of the United States on January 25. She is the first major-party
black candidate and the first woman to run for the Democratic presidential nomination.

FEBRUARY 2

Protesters in Dublin, Ireland, set fire to the
British Embassy in retaliation for Bloody Sunday.

FEBRUARY 3

The 1972 Winter Olympics open in Sapporo, Japan.

FEBRUARY 4

"One's on the Way" by Loretta Lynn is the top country single in America.

FEBRUARY 5

Influential American poet Marianne Moore dies at 84.

FEBRUARY 6

In advance of his trip to China, President Nixon secretly
asks the Chinese government to arrange a meeting with
Le Duc Tho, the lead peace negotiator for North Vietnam.

FEBRUARY 7

President Nixon signs the Federal Election Campaign Act
into law, creating the Federal Election Committee and mandating
increased disclosure of contributions to campaigns for federal office.

FEBRUARY 8

In an address before Congress, President Nixon calls
for an increase in pro-environmental legislation.

FEBRUARY 9

Paul McCartney plays his first public concert since
touring with the Beatles in 1966. He is backed by his
new band, Wings, at the University of Nottingham, England.

FEBRUARY 10

David Bowie opens his "Ziggy Stardust" tour in Tolworth, a London suburb.

FEBRUARY 11

Al Green has a number one hit with "Let's Stay Together."

FEBRUARY 12

The number one country single in America
is Faron Young's "It's Four in the Morning."

FEBRUARY 13

Led Zeppelin must cancel a concert in Singapore because government
officials will not allow the band to leave the plane due to their long hair.

FEBRUARY 14

The animated TV version of Dr. Seuss's *The Lorax,* a children's book
warning of the dangers of pollution and deforestation, airs on CBS.

FEBRUARY 15

Dutch physician Willem J. Kolff is granted a U.S. patent for the first artificial heart.

FEBRUARY 16

John Lennon and Yoko Ono are the co-hosts this week on *The Mike Douglas Show.*

FEBRUARY 17

The Volkswagen Beetle surpasses the Ford Model T
as the most mass-produced automobile in history.

On January 30, 27 unarmed civilians are shot by the British Army during a civil rights march in
Derry, Ireland; 14 die. They are pictured in this mural, one of many in Derry commemorating
the Troubles in Northern Ireland.

FEBRUARY 18

The California Supreme Court rules the death penalty unconstitutional, commuting the sentences of 102 death row inmates to life imprisonment.

FEBRUARY 19

Black entertainer Sammy Davis Jr. kisses the bigoted Archie Bunker on the cheek in what is arguably the most famous episode of the CBS sitcom *All in the Family.*

FEBRUARY 20

Walter Winchell, the once-powerful (and feared) New York gossip columnist and narrator of the TV crime drama *The Untouchables,* dies at age 74.

FEBRUARY 21

President Nixon arrives in Beijing (then called Peking), becoming the first American president to visit China and ending 22 years of hostile relations between the two nations.

FEBRUARY 22

First Lady Pat Nixon visits the Peking Zoo, where she admires the giant pandas. Later in the year the Chinese government will make a gift of two pandas to the National Zoo in the First Lady's honor.

FEBRUARY 23

The Environmental Protection Agency (EPA) orders that unleaded gasoline be made available at all gas stations in America, the beginning of the phasing out of leaded gas.

FEBRUARY 24

North Vietnamese negotiators walk out of the Paris Peace Talks in protest against recent heavy American bombing.

FEBRUARY 25

Paul McCartney releases a controversial but popular single, "Give Ireland Back to the Irish."

FEBRUARY 26

In Logan County, West Virginia, 125 people are killed when a coal slurry containment dam bursts, four days after inspectors had pronounced it safe.

FEBRUARY 27

The "Shanghai Communiqué" is drafted, stating points of accord between the American and Chinese governments, such as a mutual desire to keep the Soviet Union in check, and points of difference, such as on Taiwanese autonomy.

FEBRUARY 28

President Nixon and his entourage return to the United States. Nixon's trip to China will be considered the highlight of his presidency.

FEBRUARY 29

The year 1972 becomes the longest in history as two leap-seconds are added by the International Earth Rotation and Reference Systems Service, instead of the usual one leap-second.

MARCH 1

Congress approves the Clean Water Act of 1972.

MARCH 2

The deep-space probe *Pioneer 10* is launched. The craft carries a plaque engraved with a message for aliens who might intercept it. The probe would fly by Jupiter in 1973 and leave the solar system in 1983, the first man-made object ever to do so.

MARCH 3

"Bedtime Story" is a number one country hit for Tammy Wynette.

MARCH 4

California lowers the age of adulthood from 21 to 18.

National security advisor (and soon to be secretary of state) Henry A. Kissinger.

MARCH 5

"Without You" by Nilsson is number one on the pop singles chart.

MARCH 6

John Lennon's visa to remain in the United States is revoked over a 1968 drug-possession misdemeanor in London. It is later revealed that the Nixon administration initiated the proceedings for fear that Lennon's anti-war activities could disrupt Nixon's reelection campaign, and Lennon's deportation order is overturned.

MARCH 7

TWA airline receives an anonymous phone call warning of time bombs placed on four of its passenger jets, with a demand of 2 million dollars. One flight, en route from New York to Los Angeles, is called back to Kennedy Airport, where police find a bomb loaded with C4 explosives and defuse it with 12 minutes to spare.

MARCH 8

A second bomb explodes on board a TWA jet on the ground in Las Vegas after two police searches fail to find it. Fortunately the jet is empty when the bomb destroys it.

MARCH 9

Freddie Hart scores a number one country hit with "My Hang-Up Is You."

MARCH 10

Radio personality Larry King is cleared of larceny charges, levied by a former business partner, which led to his arrest the previous December.

MARCH 11

Carnival Cruise Lines dispatches its first ship, the *Mardi Gras,* on an eight-day maiden voyage from Miami, Florida, whereupon it runs aground on a sandbar and must be towed back out to sea. The publicity doesn't appear to hurt Carnival, and the passengers never stopped partying.

MARCH 12

Australia withdraws its troops from South Vietnam.

MARCH 13

Author Clifford Irving pleads guilty to fraud and larceny charges for writing a fake autobiography of tycoon Howard Hughes and selling it to McGraw-Hill Publishing and *Time* magazine.

MARCH 14

California governor Ronald Reagan pardons country singer Merle Haggard for all past crimes, including a 1957 robbery in Bakersfield.

MARCH 15

Francis Ford Coppola's film *The Godfather* opens. It would
go on to make more money than any motion picture had
before—$87.5 million—and would hold that record until 1975.

MARCH 16

President Nixon calls for a moratorium on "forced busing,"
the practice of transporting students into other school
districts in order to desegregate those districts.

MARCH 17

Director John Waters premieres his infamous film
Pink Flamingos at the University of Baltimore, Maryland.

MARCH 18

Neil Young's "Heart of Gold" is the number one pop single in the country.

MARCH 19

After a long legal battle over due credit, a U.S. court rules that John
Vincent Atanasoff is the inventor of the electronic digital computer.

MARCH 20

White House officials John Mitchell and Jeb Magruder
discuss G. Gordon Liddy's proposal to bug the offices
of the Democratic National Committee. Magruder
contacts chief of staff H.R. Haldeman, who
confirms that the president approves of the plan.

President Richard Nixon and Premier Zhou Enlai of share a toast on February 25, during the president's historic visit to China.

MARCH 21

The U.S. Supreme Court strikes down Tennessee's year-long
residency requirement for voting as unconstitutional.

MARCH 22

A congressional panel, the National Commission on Marihauna and Drug
Abuse, unanimously (and startlingly) recommends the decriminalization
of marijuana for private use. The panel's recommendation is not taken up.

MARCH 23

Scientists and the media arrive in the Philippines to meet the Tasady, a
tribe of cave dwellers so isolated that they have not progressed since the
Stone Age. Fourteen years later the tribe is revealed to be an elaborate hoax.

MARCH 24

British prime minister Edward Heath disbands the parliament
of Northern Ireland and imposes direct rule from London.

MARCH 25

"Rock and Roll Lullaby" by B.J. Thomas tops the adult-contemporary singles chart.

MARCH 26

Rolling Stone Keith Richards and girlfriend Anita Pallenberg check into a Swiss clinic to clean up their mutual addiction to heroin.

MARCH 27

M.C. Escher, the Dutch artist famous for his lithographs of elaborate optical illusions, dies at age 73.

MARCH 28

Barbara Jordan becomes the first black woman to head a legislature as she is elected president *pro tempore* of the Texas State Senate. On June 10 the position would call for her to be acting governor in the absence of the sitting governor and lieutenant governor, who are out of the state.

MARCH 29

East Germany opens the Berlin Wall to allow visitors from the west unfettered travel access throughout the country for eight days, the first time this has been permitted in 20 years.

MARCH 30

North Vietnamese forces launch a seven-month offensive to capture South Vietnam's Quang Tri province.

MARCH 31

In Scotland, police stop a team of monster hunters who have removed the carcass of a large animal from Loch Ness. The carcass turns out to be a recently dead elephant seal that had been brought to the lake as a practical joke.

APRIL 1

The Major League Baseball Players' Association calls a strike over a dispute with owners regarding player pensions, delaying the start of the season.

APRIL 2

New York Mets manager Gil Hodges dies at age 47.

APRIL 3

Charlie Chaplin, 82, returns to the States to appear at the Academy Awards, the first time he has been in the country in 20 years after expatriating to France.

APRIL 4

Adam Clayton Powell Jr., the first African-American congressman from New York and a powerful voice in Congress, dies at age 63.

APRIL 5

A rare tornado in the Pacific Northwest reaches F3 status and cuts a swath of destruction from Portland, Oregon to Vancouver, Washington.

On February 21, President Nixon meets with China's Communist Party Leader, Mao Tse-Tung.

APRIL 6

More than 400 American planes saturation-bomb North Vietnamese targets in retaliation for the invasion of Quang Tri.

APRIL 7

"Crazy" Joey Gallo, enforcer for the Profaci crime family, is gunned down in a restaurant in Little Italy, New York, on his 43rd birthday. Gallo was known for his active trigger finger, and his exploits were the basis for several of the incidents portrayed in Mario Puzo's *The Godfather*.

APRIL 8

"A Horse With No Name" by America is the number one pop single in the country.

APRIL 9

Golfer Jack Nicklaus wins the Masters Tournament in Augusta, Georgia.

APRIL 10

The United States, the Soviet Union, and 70 other nations enter an agreement to ban the development of biological weapons.

APRIL 11

For the first time, the press is allowed to sit in on a meeting of Catholic bishops of the United States. Unfortunately, the meeting is conducted entirely in Latin.

APRIL 12

The Major League Baseball players' strike ends. The season will be short as the missed games will not be rescheduled.

APRIL 13

The Senate approves the War Powers Act, which gives the president the authority to mobilize troops without congressional approval.

APRIL 14

The Irish Republican Army sets off 14 bombs in Belfast, Northern Ireland, to commemorate the 14 who died on "Bloody Sunday."

APRIL 15

Investigative reporter Jack Anderson receives a letter from a White House source tipping him off about the proposed plan to wiretap Democratic National Committee phones at the Watergate Hotel. Anderson ignores the tip.

APRIL 16

Ling-Ling and Hsing-Hsing arrive at the National Zoo in Washington, D.C. The giant pandas, the first ever to appear in the United States, are a gift from China and a huge attraction for the zoo over the next two decades.

APRIL 17

Demonstrators converge on the University of Maryland campus to stage the first antiwar protest of the year, focusing on the university's Reserve Officers Training Corps (ROTC). The National Guard is called in and hundreds of student protesters are arrested.

APRIL 18

For the first time, female runners' times are acknowledged in the Boston Marathon.

APRIL 19

The first organized storm-chasers, a team from the University of Oklahoma, go into the field, chasing a cyclone near Davis, Oklahoma, to collect data.

APRIL 20

U.S. National Security Adviser Henry Kissinger arrives in Moscow for secret talks with Soviet leader Leonid Brezhnev and foreign minister Andrei Gromyko.

APRIL 21

Sweden becomes the first country to legally recognize transgendered persons.

Apollo 16 lifts off from Kennedy Space center on April 16. It is the 10th manned mission in the Apollo space program, and when it lands on the Moon it will be the fifth Apollo mission to do so.

APRIL 22

Jerry Lee Lewis's cover of the Big Bopper's "Chantilly Lace" tops the country charts.

APRIL 23

Astronauts on the *Apollo 16* mission explore the
highland area of the moon for the first time.

APRIL 24

UNESCO passes a resolution prohibiting the import and export
of cultural property between nations, in an effort to stop the
export of national treasures and native plants and animals.

APRIL 25

The Polaroid SX-70 camera, capable of producing
photos that self-develop within minutes, is introduced.

APRIL 26

President Nixon announces the imminent withdrawal of
20,000 ground troops from South Vietnam. He will, concurrently,
double the number of warships deployed to the conflict.

Day-by-Day Calendar of 1972 51

APRIL 27

Alene B. Duerk is made the United States Navy's first female admiral.

APRIL 28

Joseph L. Brady, an astronomer at the Lawrence Livermore National Laboratory, announces that his calculations of gravitational data point to the existence of a tenth planet, larger than Saturn, in our solar system. His theory will be rejected after further study.

APRIL 29

New York mayor John Lindsay announces his public support for John Lennon in his fight to remain in the United States.

APRIL 30

After 27 years on the air, the CBS radio variety program *Arthur Godfrey Time* airs for the last time. Godfrey signs off and retires from broadcasting.

MAY 1

Quang Tri province is captured by the North Vietnamese.

MAY 2

J. Edgar Hoover, director of the Federal Bureau of Investigation since its inception, dies at age 77. L. Patrick Gray is appointed his successor.

MAY 3

The Grateful Dead perform at the Olympia Theater in Greece. The recording of this show ends up as part of *Europe '72*, the band's best-selling live album and regarded by fans as their best.

MAY 4

The United States and South Vietnam pull out of the Paris Peace Talks, citing a lack of progress in negotiations with North Vietnam.

MAY 5

Blues pioneer the Reverend Gary Davis dies at age 76.

MAY 6

Riva Ridge wins the Kentucky Derby.

MAY 7

The Los Angeles Lakers beat the New York Knicks 114–106 to win
the NBA championship in game five of the best-of-seven series.

Future Atlanta Braves third baseman Chipper Jones is born on April 24 in DeLand, Florida.

MAY 8

President Nixon announces the dropping of mines into Haiphong harbor, North Vietnam's largest port.

MAY 9

The Humble Oil Company changes its familiar trademark name from ESSO to EXXON.

MAY 10

Cat Stevens's "Morning Has Broken" is the top adult-contemporary single.

MAY 11

The Boston Bruins beat the New York Rangers 3–0 in game 6 of the National Hockey League Championship series to win the Stanley Cup.

MAY 12

"Grandma Harp" by Merle Haggard is the number one country single in the United States.

MAY 13

The United States deploys its new weapon, a laser-guided bomb, to destroy the Thanh Hoa Bridge in North Vietnam.

MAY 14

Center fielder Willie Mays, traded by the San Francisco Giants to the New York Mets on May 11, hits the game-winning home run against his former team. The Mets win, 5–4.

MAY 15

While campaigning for president in Maryland, Alabama governor George Wallace is shot five times by a would-be assassin. As a result of the shooting, Wallace is permanently paralyzed from the waist down.

MAY 16

In a game between the Philadelphia Phillies and the Chicago Cubs, the Phillies' Greg Luzinski hits a 500-foot homer that strikes the replica of the Liberty Bell at the far end of Veterans Stadium, the only player ever to accomplish that feat.

MAY 17

The Ohio College Library Center begins to link its computer network with libraries in other states, creating a national network that now links over 60,000 libraries as the Online Computer Library Center.

MAY 18

The Sea-Bed Treaty, a 1971 international accord prohibiting the placement of nuclear weapons installations on the ocean floor, goes into effect.

MAY 19

A bomb placed inside a women's restroom inside the Pentagon explodes. No one is harmed.

MAY 20

Roberta Flack has the number one pop single in America with "The First Time Ever I Saw Your Face."

MAY 21

At St. Peter's Basilica in the Vatican, a Hungarian geologist named Laszlo Toth suddenly cries out "I am Jesus Christ, risen from the dead!" and begins vandalizing Michelangelo's *Pieta* with a hammer, doing extensive damage to the 475-year-old sculpture before bystanders pull him away.

MAY 22

President Nixon becomes the first U.S. president to visit Moscow as he arrives for a summit meeting with Soviet first secretary Leonid Brezhnev.

MAY 23

The Rolling Stones release *Exile on Main Street*,
widely considered the best album of their long career.

J. Edgar Hoover, the first director of the Federal Bureau of Investigation (pictured here in
the Oval Office in 1967), dies on May 2.

MAY 24

The United States and the Soviet Union agree to begin the
Apollo-Soyuz project, a proposed joint venture in space.

MAY 25

"Oh Girl" by the Chi-Lites takes the number one spot on the pop charts.

MAY 26

President Nixon and Secretary Brezhnev sign the Strategic Arms Limitations Treaty
(SALT), which calls for both nations to stop production of new nuclear missiles.

MAY 27

Conway Twitty tops the country charts with "(Lost Her Love) on Our Last Date."

MAY 28

After a botched attempt two days earlier, a team of burglars working
for the Committee to Re-Elect the President (CRP, or sometimes
known as CREEP) manages to place wiretaps on phones in the
Democratic National Committee's offices in the Watergate Hotel.

MAY 29

Moe Berg—baseball catcher, Princeton Law graduate, and OSS spy—dies at age 70.

MAY 30

Mark Donohue wins the Indianapolis 500.

MAY 31

Dr. Walter Freeman, inventor of the controversial transorbital (or "ice pick") lobotomy, whose patients included Rosemary Kennedy, dies at age 76.

JUNE 1

Pablo Picasso finishes *The Embrace,* his final painting.

JUNE 2

The Staple Singers hit number one on the pop charts with "I'll Take You There."

JUNE 3

Donna Fargo's "The Happiest Girl in the Whole
U.S.A." is the top country single in America.

JUNE 4

After a highly publicized and tense trial, black activist Angela Davis is acquitted
of charges stemming from the kidnapping and murder of a judge in 1970.

JUNE 5

The United Nations Conference on the Human Environment, designed to raise
awareness of the need for global environmentalism, convenes for the first time.
Beginning in 1973, this day will be designated World Environment Day.

JUNE 6

IBM Corporation receives a U.S. patent for the "floppy
disk," a data-storage unit for its computers.

JUNE 7

Grease opens on Broadway. The musical about romance between
bad boys and good girls in the 1950s would run until 1980,
spinning off a wildly successful feature film along the way.

JUNE 8

One of the most iconic photographs of the Vietnam War is taken, of a nine-year-old South Vietnamese girl named Phan Thi Kim Phuc running naked down a road after being burned in a mistaken napalm attack on her village by friendly forces.

On June 17, five men are apprehended in side Democratic National Committee headquarters in the Watergate building (pictured here). The ensuing scandal would lead to the resignation of President Richard Nixon.

JUNE 9

A struggling New Jersey singer-songwriter named
Bruce Springsteen signs a 10-record deal with CBS Records.

JUNE 10

Elvis Presley performs the first of four sold-out
shows in Madison Square Garden, New York.

JUNE 11

Kathy Ahern wins the 18th LPGA Championship.

JUNE 12

Loaded with songs about the Attica riots and the Irish situation, among
others, John Lennon's most political album, *Sometime in NYC,* hits stores.

JUNE 13

Clyde McPhatter, influential R&B artist and leader of the
Drifters, dies at age 39. He would be posthumously
inducted into the Rock and Roll Hall of Fame 15 years later.

JUNE 14

The Environmental Protection Agency orders an
immediate ban on the use of the pesticide DDT.

JUNE 15

Yachtsman Dougal Robertson and his family are forced to
abandon their vessel when it is attacked by killer whales.
The family will drift on the Pacific Ocean for the next
38 days before being rescued. Robertson will detail
his family's ordeal in a book, *Survive the Savage Sea*.

JUNE 16

The Federal Communications Commission allows private companies to
build their own ground systems for the use of satellite transmissions.
This action will jumpstart the growth of cable television networks.

JUNE 17

After one of its wiretaps fails, the five-man team of burglars returns to the
Democratic National Committee's offices in the Watergate Hotel in an attempt
to fix the problem. This time they are caught and arrested, kicking off the
chain of events that will lead to President Nixon's resignation in 1974.

JUNE 18

The U.S. Supreme Court rules against St. Louis Cardinals center fielder
Curt Flood in his lawsuit against Major League Baseball over Flood's
refusal to accept a trade to the Philadelphia Phillies and his subsequent
loss of income. Although the league had adopted free agency after
five years of service in 1970 (the "Curt Flood rule"), the court found
that at the time Flood had no legal standing to refuse the trade.

JUNE 19

The U.S. Supreme Court rules that the federal government
does not have the right to spy on private citizens without
a warrant, ending years of Justice Department wiretapping.

JUNE 20

President Nixon and his chief of staff, H.R. Haldeman, meet for two hours
in the Oval Office. Prosecutors investigating the Watergate scandal will ask for
the tape of that meeting and find that 18-1/2 minutes of tape have been erased.

JUNE 21

Sammy Davis Jr.'s rendition of "The Candy Man"
is the number one pop single in America.

JUNE 22

The one-millionth Ford Thunderbird rolls off the assembly line.

JUNE 23

During a meeting with chief of staff Haldeman, President Nixon orders that the
FBI be instructed to halt its investigation of the Watergate break-in. When this
Oval Office tape is heard, it will be the "smoking gun" that causes Nixon to resign.

JUNE 24

"That's Why I Love You Like I Do" is another in a long line
of number one country singles for Sonny James.

JUNE 25

Alfred Baldwin, the CRP operative who had been listening to conversations
obtained via the wiretaps at the Watergate Hotel, comes forward with an
offer to testify about the plan in exchange for immunity from prosecution.

Senator (and soon-to-be Democratic presidential nominee) George McGovern speaks during
the run-up to the 1972 Democratic National Convention.

JUNE 26

Roberto Duran knocks out Ken Buchanan
at Madison Square Garden to become
world lightweight champion. Duran will hold
that title until 1979, but will move on to
become champ in the next three weight
classes throughout the 1980s.

JUNE 27

The videogame company Atari is incorporated in California.

JUNE 28

Hank Williams Jr. takes the top country spot with "Eleven Roses."

JUNE 29

The U.S. Supreme Court, deciding 5–4 in favor
of the plaintiff in *Furman v. Georgia,* rules that
all existing state death-penalty laws are
unconstitutional and calls for an immediate
moratorium of state executions. State legislatures
will go to work revising their death-penalty statutes,
but their will be no executions anywhere
in the United States for five years.

JUNE 30

After four years of litigation and a scandal that disqualified the first-place winner, Forward Pass is declared the winner of the 1968 Kentucky Derby.

JULY 1

Former attorney general John Mitchell leaves his current post as the head of the CRP, citing personal reasons.

JULY 2

India and Pakistan sign the Simla Agreement, a nonaggression pact designed to ease relations between the two nations in the aftermath of their 1971 border war.

JULY 3

Mississippi Fred McDowell, blues artist, dies at age 68.

JULY 4

Secretariat makes his racing debut at Aqueduct. The two-year-old racehorse places fourth, the worst finish of his career. He would go on to win the Triple Crown in 1973.

JULY 5

The United States calls off a top-secret program called "Operation Popeye," an attempt to hinder enemy forces by seeding clouds over Vietnam, Laos, and Cambodia. The program is suspended because of environmental concerns.

JULY 6

Through the CRP, the Watergate burglars receive the first installment of "hush money" in exchange for not implicating the White House in their activities. They will eventually be paid over $400,000.

JULY 7

The FBI admits its first two female agents.

JULY 8

The United States agrees to sell grain to the Soviet Union, which faces an agricultural shortfall, for $750 million over three years.

JULY 9

British soldiers kill five civilians in Belfast, ending a ceasefire with the Irish Republican Army.

JULY 10

A total solar eclipse occurs over the Pacific Ocean,
visible from the American Northwest.

JULY 11

A highly publicized chess match between the reigning world champion,
Boris Spassky (USSR), and the U.S. champion Bobby Fischer begins
in Reykjavik, Iceland, nine days later than scheduled. Even so, Fischer
is late for the match, and Spassky makes the first move without him.

Future actor Benjamin Géza Affleck-Boldt (shown here during a USO-sponsored tour
of the USS Enterprise) is born on August 15 in Berkeley, California. His stage name
would be shortened to "Ben Affleck."

JULY 12

Buck Owens's "Made in Japan" is the number one country single in America.

JULY 13

South Dakota senator George McGovern receives his party's nomination for president at the Democratic National Convention in Miami, Florida.

JULY 14

Because of delays in nominating Thomas Eagleton as his running mate, Senator McGovern is not able to give his acceptance speech until 2:30 am Eastern Time.

JULY 15

Actress Jane Fonda sets off a firestorm of criticism when she poses with a North Vietnamese anti-aircraft gun in Hanoi. She will be known and vilified by many in America as "Hanoi Jane" even to this day.

JULY 16

Thomas Eboli, head of the Genovese crime family, is shot and killed in Brooklyn.

JULY 17

The USS *Warrington* is destroyed by underwater mines in the Gulf of Tonkin, presumed by many to be American mines adrift from their initial placement in North Vietnamese ports. She will be the only American warship lost in the Vietnam War.

JULY 18

Egyptian President Anwar Sadat severs his military partnership with the Soviet Union, ordering over 20,000 Soviet personnel to leave the country.

JULY 19

American and North Vietnamese negotiators return to the table at the Paris Peace Talks.

JULY 20

Jane Fonda holds a press conference to defend her visit to North Vietnam, accusing President Nixon of genocidal tactics by ordering saturation bombing against the North.

JULY 21

Bill Withers's "Lean on Me" is the number one pop single in the country.

JULY 22

Charley Pride has a number one country hit
with "It's Gonna Take a Little Bit Longer."

JULY 23

The first Earth Resources Technology Satellite, later renamed
Landsat, is launched. The satellite is designed to pass over
all parts of the Earth and transmit high-resolution images.

JULY 24

Pharmacologists at Eli Lilly conduct the first tests on the compound
that will eventually be marketed as the antidepressant Prozac.

JULY 25

Democratic vice presidential candidate Thomas Eagleton reveals to the press that
he had been under psychiatric care three times and had received electroshock
therapy. Despite the endorsement of his running mate, George McGovern,
Eagleton's revelations seriously compromise his party's confidence.

JULY 26

Photographer Diane Arbus commits suicide at age 48.

JULY 27

McDonnell-Douglas Aircraft introduces the F-15 Eagle fighter jet, which will become the standard fighter for the United States Air Force.

JULY 28

Editorials run in the *New York Times, Washington Post, Los Angeles Times,* and *Baltimore Sun* urging Thomas Eagleton to step down as the Democratic vice presidential candidate.

On September 5, eight Palestinian terrorists capture and kill 11 Israeli athletes, coaches, and officials during the Olympic Games in Munich. Pictured is a memorial located in Ben-Shemen forest in Israel.

JULY 29

The Soviet Union makes its second attempt to launch a
space station into orbit. The mission fails when a second-
stage rocket misfires and the station falls into the Pacific Ocean.

JULY 30

The Associated Press begins a news exchange with China's
Xinhua News Agency, marking the first time an American news
organization has been given open access inside China in 22 years.

JULY 31

Thomas Eagleton resigns from the Democratic presidential ticket.
He will be replaced as Senator McGovern's running mate by Sargent
Shriver, founder of the Peace Corps and U.S. ambassador to France.

AUGUST 1

Washington Post reporters Carl Bernstein and Bob Woodward break the first story
about Republican campaign funds being funneled to the Watergate burglars.

AUGUST 2

A check from the CRP is discovered to have been deposited in the
bank account of Bernard Barker, one of the Watergate burglars.

AUGUST 3

The U.S. Senate ratifies the Anti-Ballistic Missile Treaty between America and the Soviet Union. The treaty limits the number and locations of such missiles on both sides.

AUGUST 4

Arthur Bremer is sentenced to 63 years in prison for the attempted assassination of Alabama governor George Wallace.

AUGUST 5

Sargent Shriver is confirmed as George McGovern's running mate after five other prospective candidates refuse.

AUGUST 6

Atlanta Brave Hank Aaron knocks out his 660th and 661st home runs, setting a record for most homers by a player for a single team.

AUGUST 7

The most powerful solar flare ever measured is seen from Earth.

AUGUST 8

For the first time, women are permitted to serve
in active operations in the United States Navy.

AUGUST 9

"Bless Your Heart" by Freddie Hart tops the country charts.

AUGUST 10

A meteor passes within 36 miles of Earth and
is visible in the afternoon sky over Canada.

AUGUST 11

The last American ground combat troops are pulled out of
South Vietnam, though air and sea operations continue.

AUGUST 12

Negotiators from the Paris Peace Talks reveal to the press
that President Nixon had an opportunity to end the
Vietnam War in 1969 and refused to explore that option.

AUGUST 13

Former attorney general Ramsey Clark returns from a fact-finding trip to North Vietnam and discloses that American bombing raids have hit hospitals and other civilian targets.

AUGUST 14

Oscar Levant, concert pianist famous for his flamboyant persona and appearances in films, dies at age 65.

One of the last of the American muscle cars, the Chevelle begins to settle into a more family-oriented design around 1972.

AUGUST 15

Woody Allen's comedy (very loosely based on the book) *Everything You Ever Wanted to Know About Sex (But Were Afraid to Ask)* is in movie theaters.

AUGUST 16

Moroccan rebels, led by Defense Minister Mohammed Oufkir, attempt a royal *coup d'etat,* sending air force planes to shoot down the jet carrying King Hassan II back to Morocco from a meeting in France. The king survives the attack, the coup attempt is foiled, and the next day Oufkir is found dead from a questionable suicide.

AUGUST 17

South Carolina bluesman Baby Tate dies at age 56.

AUGUST 18

Gilbert O'Sullivan has a number one pop single with "Alone Again (Naturally)."

AUGUST 19

The Midnight Special debuts on NBC. Actually airing at 1:00 am, the show features live (not pre-recorded) musical performances from contemporary rock artists as well as older nostalgia footage and stand-up comedians. The pilot aired as an effort to encourage young people to vote in the upcoming presidential election and featured such performers as War, Linda Ronstadt, Harry Chapin, and comedian Andy Kaufman.

AUGUST 20

Miami, Florida, police investigate the attempted bombing
of a car at the Republican National Convention. It is believed
that the car's owner, a Cuban journalist, was targeted
because of a pro-Nixon editorial he had written.

AUGUST 21

The satellite *Copernicus,* an orbiting space telescope, is launched.

AUGUST 22

In Brooklyn, three men attempt to rob a branch of the Chase
Manhattan Bank only to find that most of the cash has already been
shipped out by armored car. The robbers' bad luck continues when
police arrive just as they are leaving the building. The resulting standoff
will be the subject of the 1975 film *Dog Day Afternoon* with Al Pacino.

AUGUST 23

"Brandy (You're a Fine Girl)" takes the number one spot on the pop singles chart.

AUGUST 24

"If You Leave Me Tonight I'll Cry" is a number one country hit for Jerry Wallace.

AUGUST 25

Wal-Mart begins trading shares on the New York Stock Exchange.

AUGUST 26

The 1972 Summer Olympics opens in Munich, West Germany.

AUGUST 27

President Nixon hosts an all-star party at his home in San Clemente, California. Over 400 celebrities attend, including John Wayne, Frank Sinatra, and actress Jill St. John, who is dating national security adviser Henry Kissinger at the time.

AUGUST 28

Air Force Captain R. Stephen Ritchie downs his fifth North Vietnamese MiG fighter, making him the first American flying ace of the Vietnam War.

AUGUST 29

President Nixon announces more troop withdrawals from South Vietnam. The proposal would constitute a 95% draw-down from peak deployment of over 500,000 American troops.

AUGUST 30

John Lennon and Yoko Ono, as well as Stevie Wonder and Roberta Flack, perform at a benefit concert at Madison Square Garden, proceeds of which are to benefit mentally disabled children.

AUGUST 31

The United States reports the lowest weekly troop casualty figures (five dead) of the Vietnam War.

As the ticker tape flies during a campaign motorcade in Atlanta, Georgia, on October 12, Pat Nixon reaches out to a little girl from her car.

SEPTEMBER 1

Bobby Fischer wins the World Chess Championship in Reykjavik, Iceland, defeating Boris Spassky of the Soviet Union in the 21st game between them.

SEPTEMBER 2

Don Gibson's "Woman (Sensuous Woman)" tops the country charts.

SEPTEMBER 3

Three downed American pilots are released, the first POWs to be returned by North Vietnam in three years.

SEPTEMBER 4

American swimmer Mark Spitz becomes the first athlete to win seven gold medals in a single Olympics.

SEPTEMBER 5

Members of a Palestinian terrorist group called Black September storm the Olympic Village, kill two Israeli athletes, and hold nine others hostage, beginning what would become known as the Munich Massacre.

SEPTEMBER 6

Black September moves their hostages to
Furstenfeldbruck Airport. A failed rescue
attempt by West German police results
in the deaths of all hostages, five of
the terrorists, and one police officer.

SEPTEMBER 7

Prime Minister Indira Gandhi approves the
development of nuclear weapons in India.

SEPTEMBER 8

The Israeli air force bombs Palestinian compounds in Syria
and Lebanon in retaliation for the events in Munich.

SEPTEMBER 9

The U.S. men's basketball team loses 51–50 to the
Soviet Union in the Munich Olympics, due
to a last-second Soviet goal after Olympic
officials added three seconds to the clock.
Protesting that they had won in regulation time,
the American team refuses the silver medal.

SEPTEMBER 10

Romanian tennis player Ilie Nastase wins his first and only U.S. Open Men's Singles championship, defeating Arthur Ashe. The day before, Billie Jean King won the Women's Singles title, the first year that female players received the same prize money as men.

SEPTEMBER 11

San Francisco's Bay Area Rapid Transit system (BART) goes into operation.

SEPTEMBER 12

"Black and White" by Three Dog Night tops the pop charts.

SEPTEMBER 13

"When the Snow Is on the Roses" by Sonny James is the number one country hit in America.

SEPTEMBER 14

The Waltons, a family drama set in rural Virginia during the Great Depression, begins its 10-year run on CBS.

SEPTEMBER 15

The Watergate burglars are indicted, along with G. Gordon Liddy
and CIA operative E. Howard Hunt. White House counsel
John Dean meets with the president and the chief of staff, and
the conversation turns to retaliation against President Nixon's enemies.

SEPTEMBER 16

A *Washington Post* reporter receives confirmation from his secret
informer, "Deep Throat," that funds from the Nixon reelection campaign
were used to finance the Watergate burglaries. Deep Throat would
eventually reveal himself to be FBI associate director W. Mark Felt.

Visible from the gunner's position in the air over Vietnam is a U.S. Air Force Sikorsky HH-53
Super Jolly Green Giant helicopter of the 40th Aerospace Rescue and Recovery Squadron.

SEPTEMBER 17

*M*A*S*H,* a sitcom set in an army hospital camp during the Korean War, premieres. It would run for 11 years. The Korean War lasted three years.

SEPTEMBER 18

Art Williams, Major League Baseball's first black umpire, calls his first game, Los Angeles vs. San Diego.

SEPTEMBER 19

Black September, the Palestinian terror group behind the Munich Massacre, assassinates Israeli agricultural consultant Dr. Ami Shachori with one of eight letter-bombs sent to the Israeli embassy in London.

SEPTEMBER 20

Heavyweight boxer Floyd Patterson gives up on his quest to regain the title after Muhammad Ali defeats him in seven rounds.

SEPTEMBER 21

Philippines president Ferdinand Marcos responds to recent terrorist attacks by declaring martial law.

SEPTEMBER 22

David Bowie launches his first American tour, in support of
The Rise and Fall of Ziggy Stardust and the Spiders From Mars.

SEPTEMBER 23

Conway Twitty has a number one country hit
with his version of "I Can't Stop Loving You."

SEPTEMBER 24

One of the most memorable games in NFL history is played, between the
Baltimore Colts, led by legendary quarterback Johnny Unitas, and the New York
Jets, led by Joe Namath. Unitas passes for 376 yards and three touchdowns,
while Namath passes for 496 yards and six TDs to lead the Jets to victory, 44–34.

SEPTEMBER 25

Paul Tutmarc, musician and inventor of the electric bass guitar, dies at age 76.

SEPTEMBER 26

President Nixon signs the law enacting the Special Supplemental
Nutrition Program for Women, Infants, and Children Program
(WIC). The program provides vouchers for low-income new
and expectant mothers to purchase food and formula.

SEPTEMBER 27

Rory Storm, leader of Rory Storm and the Hurricanes, an English rock group that included a pre-Beatles Ringo Starr, dies at age 33.

SEPTEMBER 28

"I Ain't Never" is a number one country hit for Mel Tillis.

SEPTEMBER 29

Washington Post reporters Woodward and Bernstein reveal that former attorney general John Mitchell controlled a secret Republican fund used to finance spying on Democratic leadership.

SEPTEMBER 30

Pittsburgh Pirates phenom Roberto Clemente gets his 3,000th career hit. It will also be his last. Hitless for the rest of the season and postseason, Clemente will be killed in a plane crash later in the year.

OCTOBER 1

Louis Leakey, anthropologist who posited that human origins began in Africa, dies at age 69.

OCTOBER 2

"Baby, Don't Get Hooked on Me" is a number one pop hit for Mac Davis.

OCTOBER 3

The Anti-Ballistic Missile Treaty between the United States and the Soviet Union goes into effect.

The Jackson 5, the phenomenally popular singing group composed of brothers Jackie, Tito, Jermaine, Marlon, and Michael, go on air in the *Jackson 5 Show* on November 5.

OCTOBER 4

The ABC Afterschool Special, a monthly dramatic television series aimed at providing positive messages about sensitive issues for children, premieres.

OCTOBER 5

In New York, an agreement is reached between Saudi Arabia, Kuwait, Qatar, and the United Arab Emirates on one side, and Exxon, Mobil, Chevron, and Texaco, to parcel out the Arab-American Company between the four OPEC nations. The sale makes the oil companies a $500 million profit and increases OPEC's power considerably.

OCTOBER 6

A train crash near Saltillo, Mexico, kills 208 people and injures 700 more, mostly religious pilgrims.

OCTOBER 7

The New York Islanders and the Atlanta Flames, the newest expansion teams in the National Hockey League, open the season against each other. The Flames win 3–2.

OCTOBER 8

Prescott Bush, father of President George H.W. Bush and grandfather of President George W. Bush as well as a former U.S. senator from Connecticut, dies at age 77.

OCTOBER 9

Michael Jackson's "Ben" takes over the top of the pop singles chart.

OCTOBER 10

The *Washington Post* reports that the Watergate
burglary was part of a larger White House plan to gather
information on Democratic candidates for president.

OCTOBER 11

Roe v. Wade, the landmark case that would establish abortion rights for
women, is argued before the U.S. Supreme Court for the second time.

OCTOBER 12

Lady Sings the Blues, a film about blues legend Billie Holiday starring
Diana Ross, opens in theaters. It is Ross's first acting role, and she
would receive an Academy Award nomination for her performance.

OCTOBER 13

Donna Fargo's "Funny Face" is the number one country single in America.

OCTOBER 14

Kung Fu, a television drama about the adventures of a Chinese-American Shaolin priest traveling the Old West, premieres on ABC.

OCTOBER 15

Baseball great Jackie Robinson makes his final public appearance, at Game 2 of the World Series, where he throws the first pitch.

OCTOBER 16

Agents of Israel's intelligence service the Mossad shoot and kill Wael Zwaiter on the streets of Rome. Zwaiter, suspected of belonging to the Black September organization, which attacked Israeli athletes at the Munich Olympics, is the first to fall to "Operation Wrath of God."

OCTOBER 17

Congress approves the Supplemental Security Income program, which provides benefits for the elderly and disabled who are not eligible for Social Security.

OCTOBER 18

The U.S. Senate and the House of Representatives both vote to override President Nixon's veto of the Clean Water Act.

OCTOBER 19

Bernardo Bertolucci's *Last Tango in Paris,* starring Marlon Brando,
is in theaters. Although not a pornographic film, its adult
themes and situations cause it to carry an "X" rating.

OCTOBER 20

Although they still lose to the Boston Celtics, the Buffalo Braves
set a still-unbroken NBA record for scoring in a single quarter: 58 points.
The Celtics had been up by 43, but only win by 8 at the final buzzer.

The 1972 Dodge Charger is advertised as a family car "a man could buy on looks alone."

OCTOBER 21

Chuck Berry's "My Ding-a-Ling" tops the pop chart.
Amazingly, it is the only number one single of his career.

OCTOBER 22

Days after brokering a cease-fire with North Vietnamese negotiator
Le Duc Tho in Paris, U.S, national security adviser Henry Kissinger
meets with South Vietnamese president Nguyen Van Thieu in Saigon.

OCTOBER 23

The musical *Pippin*, about the hunchbacked son
of Charlemagne, begins a long run on Broadway.

OCTOBER 24

Jackie Robinson, the first black player in Major League Baseball, dies at age 53.

OCTOBER 25

The *Washington Post* reports that White House Chief of Staff H.R. Haldeman
was among those in charge of a secret fund to finance espionage,
sabotage, and "dirty tricks" during the Presidential campaign.

OCTOBER 26

National security adviser Henry Kissinger announces to the press that
a peace agreement to end the Vietnam War is close to completion,
responding to a North Vietnamese release of the terms to the global media.

OCTOBER 27

The 5,000th episode of the beloved children's TV show *Captain Kangaroo* airs.

OCTOBER 28

The Airbus A300, the first passenger jet manufactured by a European
consortium of French, German, and Spanish manufacturers, debuts. Airbus
will go on to be a major competitor to the big American aeronautics firms.

OCTOBER 29

Palestinian hijackers take over a Lufthansa jet and demand the
release of the members of Black September in custody after the
Munich Massacre. West Germany complies the following day.

OCTOBER 30

A commuter train collision at the 27th Street station
in Chicago kills 45 passengers and injures over 332 more.
It is the worst rapid-transit accident in the city's history.

OCTOBER 31

Twenty-two soldiers are killed when their helicopter is hit
by a heat-seeking missile in the last mass-casualty
incident involving American troops of the Vietnam War.

NOVEMBER 1

Ezra Pound, one of the giants of 20th-century poetry, dies in Venice, Italy, at age 87.

NOVEMBER 2

Members of the American Indian Movement (AIM) take over the Bureau of Indian
Affairs office in Washington, D.C. They will hold it for the next seven days.

NOVEMBER 3

132 sailors on board the USS *Constellation* stage the first mass mutiny
in U.S. Navy history, refusing orders after learning that many of them were
to be dishonorably discharged. None of the mutineers will face charges.

NOVEMBER 4

Merle Haggard has a number one country
single with "It's Not Love (But It's Not Bad)."

NOVEMBER 5

Reginald Owen, an English actor best known for playing Ebenezer Scrooge in the 1938 film version of *A Christmas Carol,* dies at age 85.

NOVEMBER 6

Rutgers University plays the first intercollegiate game of Ultimate Frisbee against Princeton University on the field and date on which the two schools played the first intercollegiate football game. Rutgers wins, 29–27.

Secretary of State Kissinger, President Nixon, and Major General Alexander M. Haig Jr., discuss the Vietnam situation while at Camp David.

NOVEMBER 7

President Richard M. Nixon is reelected in a landslide victory over Senator George McGovern, capturing every state except Massachusetts.

NOVEMBER 8

Home Box Office, or HBO, begins service as the world's first pay-cable television network.

NOVEMBER 9

Canada launches *Anik-1,* the world's first geostationary communications satellite, into orbit.

NOVEMBER 10

Admiral Elmo Zumwalt, chief of U.S. Naval Operations, orders the immediate acceleration of equal-opportunity initiatives within the U.S. Navy.

NOVEMBER 11

Tammy Wynette's "My Man (Understands)" tops the country charts.

NOVEMBER 12

Sports Illustrated names Miami Dolphins coach Don Shula, the first NFL coach to win 100 games in 10 seasons, Sportsman of the Year.

NOVEMBER 13

Representatives of 79 nations convene in London to sign an agreement banning the dumping of mercury, cadmium, oil, and radioactive waste into the ocean.

NOVEMBER 14

The Dow Jones Industrial Average closes above 1,000 for the first time.

NOVEMBER 15

Pope Paul VI delivers a speech in which he states definitively that Satan is not a metaphor, but an actual, personified agent of evil.

NOVEMBER 16

The U.S. Public Health Service finally shuts down the notorious "Tuskegee Experiment," in which African-American subjects in the 1940s were unknowingly exposed to syphilis and then observed.

NOVEMBER 17

Former president Juan Peron returns
to Argentina after 17 years in exile,
accompanied by his wife, Isabel. He
will be reelected president in 1973,
and his wife will succeed him after his
death the following year. The Broadway
musical *Evita* will be based on Isabel's life.

NOVEMBER 18

Danny Whitten, guitarist for Neil Young and
Crazy Horse, dies of an overdose of alcohol
and Valium at age 29. Young will write one
of his most haunting songs, "The Needle
and the Damage Done," for Whitten.

NOVEMBER 19

Talks resume over the Strategic Arms Limitation Treaty
between the United States and the Soviet Union.

NOVEMBER 20

President Nixon, after having asked every
cabinet member and agency head to
resign, removes to Camp David to begin
building his second-term administration.

NOVEMBER 21

The convictions of the "Chicago Seven," activists accused of inciting a
riot at the 1968 Democratic National Convention in Chicago, Illinois, are
overturned because of reversible error on the part of the judge in that trial.

NOVEMBER 22

Mass murderer Richard Speck is sentenced to 1,200 years in prison,
at the time the longest prison sentence ever handed down.

President Nixon is greeted by supporters at Robins Air Force Base, Georgia, on November 18.

NOVEMBER 23

The Paris Peace Talks resume but are immediately deadlocked
as North Vietnam's representative Le Duc Tho rejects Henry
Kissinger's proposal of an international supervisory force in Vietnam.

NOVEMBER 24

In Concert, a live-performance program, debuts
on ABC with a show headlined by Alice Cooper.

NOVEMBER 25

"I Can See Clearly Now" is a number one pop hit for Johnny Nash.

NOVEMBER 26

The New York Giants crush the Philadelphia Eagles
62–10, setting a team scoring record.

NOVEMBER 27

The PBS children's program *Sesame Street* introduces
Count von Count, a purple vampire who loves
to count things and then throw back
his head and laugh in dark triumph.

NOVEMBER 28

The Canadian Football Hall of Fame officially opens in Hamilton, Ontario.

NOVEMBER 29

Carl W. Stalling Jr., best known for composing the incidental music in countless classic Warner Brothers cartoons, dies at age 81.

NOVEMBER 30

In a monumental decision for the Catholic Church, Pope Paul VI replaces the Rite of Extreme Unction (the "last rites") with the Rite of Anointing and Pastoral Care of the Sick, which may be performed before the last moments of a parishioner's life.

DECEMBER 1

Gustav Schwarzenegger—trumpet player, policeman, former Nazi officer, and father of movie star and governor of California Arnold Schwarzenegger—dies at age 65.

DECEMBER 2

The Temptations have a number one pop hit with "Papa Was a Rollin' Stone."

DECEMBER 3

Spacecraft *Pioneer 10* sends the first fly-by photographs of Jupiter back to Earth.

DECEMBER 4

Harvard University's Memorial Church ordains
the first female minister in its 336-year history.

DECEMBER 5

"I Am Woman" by Helen Reddy takes over the pop charts.

DECEMBER 6

Freddie Hart scores another number one country
single with "Got the All Overs for You (All Over Me)."

DECEMBER 7

Apollo 7, the last manned mission to the moon, is launched.
On the trip astronauts are able to take a photo of the
Earth that will become iconic as "The Blue Marble."

DECEMBER 8

Israeli Mossad agents kill Palestine Liberation Organization diplomat Dr. Mahmoud Hamshari with a bomb placed inside a telephone, in retaliation for the Munich Massacre at the Olympics, which Hamshari was suspected of helping to plan.

On December 7, Apollo 17 lifts off from Kennedy Space Center bearing astronauts Cernan, Evans, and Schmitt. It is the final manned mission of the Apollo space program.

DECEMBER 9

Louella Parsons, one of the most influential of
the Hollywood gossip columnists, dies at age 91.

DECEMBER 10

The American League of Major League Baseball adopts
the designated-hitter rule, which takes the pitcher out
of the hitting lineup and replaces him with a player
who hits but does not play defense. This rule is still
the subject of heated debate among baseball fans.

DECEMBER 11

Apollo 17's lunar module *Challenger* makes the last landing on the moon.

DECEMBER 12

The first Haitian "boat people," fleeing the oppressive
Duvalier regime in that country, land on the coast of
Florida. Six years on, 1978 will see a mass exodus from Haiti.

DECEMBER 13

North Vietnam abandons the Paris Peace Talks and ignores
President Nixon's warning to return to the table within 72 hours.

DECEMBER 14

The Poseidon Adventure is the number one movie in theaters, riding a wave of "disaster films" at the box office.

DECEMBER 15

Butch Cassidy and the Sundance Kid, starring Paul Newman and Robert Redford, opens in theaters.

DECEMBER 16

The undefeated Miami Dolphins finish the regular football season by beating the Baltimore Colts, 16–0. The team will go on to win the division and conference playoffs and then Super Bowl VII, making them the only team in NFL history with a perfect season.

DECEMBER 17

"We leave as we came, and, God willing, as we shall return, with peace and hope for all mankind," says *Apollo 17* commander Gene Cernan. During the return flight, astronaut Ron Evans makes a one-and-a-half-hour spacewalk to retrieve film from one of the lunar module's instrument bays.

DECEMBER 18

In response to North Vietnam's refusal to return to the Paris Peace Talks, the United States carries out the largest aerial bombardment of the war. This would go on for 11 days, with 121 bombing runs on North Vietnamese targets in the first 24 hours.

DECEMBER 19

Apollo 17's command module splashes down in the Pacific Ocean, ending the final manned moon mission.

DECEMBER 20

Neil Simon's *The Sunshine Boys* opens on Broadway.

DECEMBER 21

The Marine Mammal Protection Act goes into effect. The act outlaws whaling by American vessels and prohibits the taking of seals except by native Aleuts, Inuits, and Eskimos.

DECEMBER 22

Singer Joan Baez and others arrive in Hanoi as part of a peace delegation carrying Christmas letters to American prisoners of war in North Vietnam.

DECEMBER 23

An earthquake measuring 6.5 on the Richter scale strikes Managua, Nicaragua, killing more than 12,000 people.

DECEMBER 24

Charles Atlas (born Angelo Siciliano), bodybuilder and creator of the Dynamic Tension exercise regimen advertised in the back of countless comic books, dies at age 80.

A U.S. Air Force B-52 Stratofortress drops bombs over Vietnam. This aircraft would fly its final combat mission on December 29, as one of the three final B-52 aircraft to bomb North Vietnam during Operation Linebacker II.

DECEMBER 25

In an effort to silence dissidents, the USSR enacts new laws prohibiting its citizens from "disseminating false or slanderous information about the Soviet Union" to foreigners.

DECEMBER 26

Harry S Truman, former president of the United States, dies in Kansas City, Missouri, at age 88.

DECEMBER 27

Billy Paul's "Me and Mrs. Jones" is the number one pop single in America.

DECEMBER 28

The number one country single is Ray Price's "She's Got to Be a Saint."

DECEMBER 29

While addressing a conference, mathematician Edward Lorenz, a pioneer in chaos theory, coins the term "butterfly effect" for the idea that a small event in one place, such as a butterfly flapping its wings, will eventually result in a huge consequence, such as a tornado, through a chain of causation.

DECEMBER 30

The 11-day bombing of North Vietnam brings that country's representatives back to the negotiating table.

DECEMBER 31

The number one song in America is "You're So Vain" by Carly Simon.

On December 11, astronaut Eugene Cernan test-drives the lunar rover on the surface of the Moon during the Apollo 17 mission.

Davy Jones, he of the recently disbanded group The Monkees, gets a one-hour ABC television special called *Pop Goes Davy Jones*. He is shown here performing with Ilene Anderson of the soul group Sunday's Child.

Pop Culture in

1972

T he year 1972 was a watershed for popular entertainment across the board. Some of the most beloved films, music, and television shows of all time, the ones we now collect on DVD and cherish on vinyl like museum relics, were new and thrilling experiences to us that year. By anyone's reckoning it was an incredible year to have a television, a radio, or a ticket to the movies.

It's said that art flourishes the most in troubled times. It's clear from looking back at the most popular diversions of 1972 that we as an audience were ready to take chances. We spent our hard-earned entertainment dollars flocking to see Mafiosi cutting throats and gunning each other down, men and women struggling to survive Nazi aggression, a capsized ocean liner, and the stalking of cold-blooded murderers. This was the year when Dirty Harry first pulled out his .44 Magnum and asked if we felt lucky, when Laurence Olivier and Michael Caine played murderous cat-and-mouse games, and when four men in canoes did battle with the elements and hidden pursuers in the trees.

On TV, a new breed of characters with deep personal flaws brought discussions of societal issues like racism and abortion and the horrors of war into our living rooms, camouflaged in sitcom trappings. Our music was becoming more complex, rock and roll albums moving further into extended thematic statements rather than just collections of tracks for dancing, and pop and country and R&B were all willing to become more personal than ever before.

In 1972 we still used our entertainments to escape, but instead of fleeing into the arms of fluff, we used our leisure time and dollars to dare Hollywood and the music industry to bring it on.

PONG

PLAYER 1   PLAYER 2

Atari's Pong, one of the first arcade video games, is released in 1972. It would go on to be released in a home version and, for decades afterward, would be a nostalgic symbol of the 1970s.

The 10 Best-Reviewed Films:
> *The Godfather*
> *Deliverance*
> *Solaris*
> *Sleuth*
> *Aguirre: The Wrath of God*
> *Cabaret*
> *Last Tango in Paris*
> *The Poseidon Adventure*
> *Everything You Always Wanted to Know about Sex (But Were Afraid to Ask)*
> *Frenzy*

Casting *The Godfather* was a nightmare for director Francis Ford Coppola. Although Coppola wanted Marlon Brando for the role of Don Vito Corleone, the studio did not. Other names suggested for the role included Laurence Olivier, Ernest Borgnine, and comedian Danny Thomas.

The 10 top-grossing films:
> *The Godfather* ($134,966,411)
> *The Poseidon Adventure* ($93,300,000)
> *What's Up, Doc?* ($66,000,000)
> *Deliverance* ($46,122,355)
> *Jeremiah Johnson* ($44,693,786)
> *Cabaret* ($42,765,000)
> *The Getaway* ($36,734,619)
> *The Legend of Boggy Creek* ($20,000,000)
> *Lady Sings the Blues* ($19,726,490)
> *Everything You Always Wanted to Know* ... ($18, 016,290)

Academy Awards:
> Best Picture: *The Godfather*
> Best Director: Bob Fosse *(Cabaret)*
> Best Actor: Marlon Brando (*The Godfather*—declined)
> Best Actress: Liza Minelli *(Cabaret)*
> Best Supporting Actor: Joel Grey *(Cabaret)*
> Best Supporting Actress: Eileen Heckart *(Butterflies Are Free)*
> Best Foreign Language Film: *The Discreet Charm of the Bourgeoisie*

Feminist, journalist, and activist Gloria Steinem answers questions at a Women's Action Alliance news conference.

Marlon Brando refused his Oscar for Best Actor, sending Native American activist Sacheen Littlefeather, in full Apache dress, to articulate his anger over the depiction of Native Americans in film and television.

The 10 highest-rated TV shows:
All in the Family (CBS)
The Flip Wilson Show (NBC)
Marcus Welby, MD (ABC)
Gunsmoke (CBS)
ABC Movie of the Week (ABC)
Sanford & Son (NBC)
Mannix (CBS)
Funny Face (CBS)
Adam-12 (NBC)
The Mary Tyler Moore Show (CBS)

The Mary Tyler Moore Show was a hard sell for the CBS network. As originally written, the show would follow Mary Richards, a recently divorced woman seeking a new life in Minneapolis. The divorce was written out because the network feared that audiences would be turned off by Moore as a divorcee after years of happy TV marriage on *The Dick Van Dyke Show.*

Emmy Awards:
Best Comedy Show: *All in the Family*
Best Drama Show: *Elizabeth R*
Best Variety Show: *The Carol Burnett Show*
Best Actor in a Comedy: Carroll O'Connor (*All in the Family*)
Best Actress in a Comedy: Jean Stapleton (*All in the Family*)
Best Actor in a Drama: Peter Falk *(Columbo)*
Best Actress in a Drama: Glenda Jackson *(Elizabeth R)*

When *All in the Family* premiered in 1971, creator Norman Lear intended Carroll O'Connor's character, the bigoted Archie Bunker, to be thoroughly unlikeable. Instead, Bunker was voted the most beloved character in TV history in a Bravo TV survey, and number five in a similar survey by *TV Guide* (Peter Falk's Lt. Columbo came in seventh).

The 10 best-selling singles:
"The First Time Ever I Saw Your Face," Roberta Flack
"Alone Again (Naturally)," Gilbert O'Sullivan
"American Pie," Don McLean
"Without You," Nilsson
"The Candy Man," Sammy Davis, Jr.

The iconic film *The Godfather* (shown here occupying the marquee of the Imperial Theatre in Toronto, Canada), is released on March 24.

"I Gotcha," Joe Tex
"Lean on Me," Bill Withers
"Baby Don't Get Hooked on Me," Mac Davis
"Brand New Key," Melanie
"Daddy Don't You Walk So Fast," Wayne Newton

Don McLean's "American Pie" has been dissected by pop-music scholars for years, with varying interpretations of the identities of the song's various characters. When McLean was asked what "American Pie" meant, he famously replied, "It means I never have to work again."

The 10 best-selling albums:
Harvest, Neil Young
Exile on Main St., The Rolling Stones
Machine Head, Deep Purple
American Pie, Don McLean
Thick as a Brick, Jethro Tull
The Rise and Fall of Ziggy Stardust and the Spiders From Mars, David Bowie
Catch Bull at Four, Cat Stevens
Honky Chateau, Elton John
Seventh Sojourn, The Moody Blues
Paul Simon, Paul Simon

Grammy Awards:
Record of the Year: "The First Time Ever I Saw Your Face," Roberta Flack
Album of the Year: *The Concert for Bangla Desh,* George Harrison, Ravi Shanker, Bob Dylan, Leon Russell, Ringo Starr, Billy Preston, Eric Clapton, and Klaus Voormann
Song of the Year: "The First Time Ever I Saw Your Face," Ewan MacColl, songwriter
Best New Artist of the Year: America
Best Pop Vocal Performance, Male: "Without You," Nilsson
Best Pop Vocal Performance, Female: "I Am Woman," Helen Reddy
Best Pop Vocal Performance by a Duo, Group, or Chorus: "Where Is the Love," Roberta Flack and Donny Hathaway

The Concert for Bangla Desh (properly "Bangladesh") was actually a pair of benefit concerts organized by former Beatle George Harrison and Ravi Shankar to raise funds for refugees from the 1971 Indian-Pakistani war that created the state, and for those deprived by devastating storms in the region. It was the first major benefit rock concert ever put together.

Credits and Acknowledgments

John Nettles wrote text; Maurice Cobbs selected images. Individual image credits are as follows.

Chapter 1. Cameron Diaz—Sharon Graphics. Shaquille O'Neal—Airman 1st Class Alex Gouchnour, U.S. Air Force. Rebecca Romijn—The Heart Truth. Brad Paisley—Official White House photo by Pete Souza.

Chapter 2. Drugstore—Frank J. Aleksandrowicz. Jewelry-store owner—David Hiser. Mother and daughter—John H. White.

Chapter 3. Astronauts on the Moon—Harrison H. Schmitt, NASA. President Nixon—White House photo. Shirley Chisholm—Thomas H. O'Halloran. Mural—Jove. Henry Kissinger—U.S. Department of State. President Nixon and Premier Zhou—Nixon Presidential Library and Museum. President Nixon and Chairman Mao—General Services Administration. Apollo 16 liftoff—NASA. Chipper Jones—Alex Brady. J. Edgar Hoover—Yoichi R. Okamoto. Watergate—Indutiomarus. George McGovern—Warren K. Leffler. Israeli Olympic memorial—Pesis. Chevrolet Chevelle—Jack Snell. Pat Nixon—White House photo. Helicopter view—Ken Hackman, USAF. Jackson 5—CBS publicity photo. Dodge Charger—Alden Jewell. Camp David meeting—Oliver F. Atkins. President Nixon, Robins AFB—Oliver F. Atkins. Apollo 17 liftoff—NASA. Bomber—U.S. Air Force. Lunar rover—Harrison H. Schmitt, NASA.

Chapter 4. Davy Jones and Ilene Anderson—ABC publicity photo. Pong—Axel Tregoning. Gloria Steinem—Warren K. Leffler. Imperial Theatre marquee—City of Toronto Archives.